I0797408

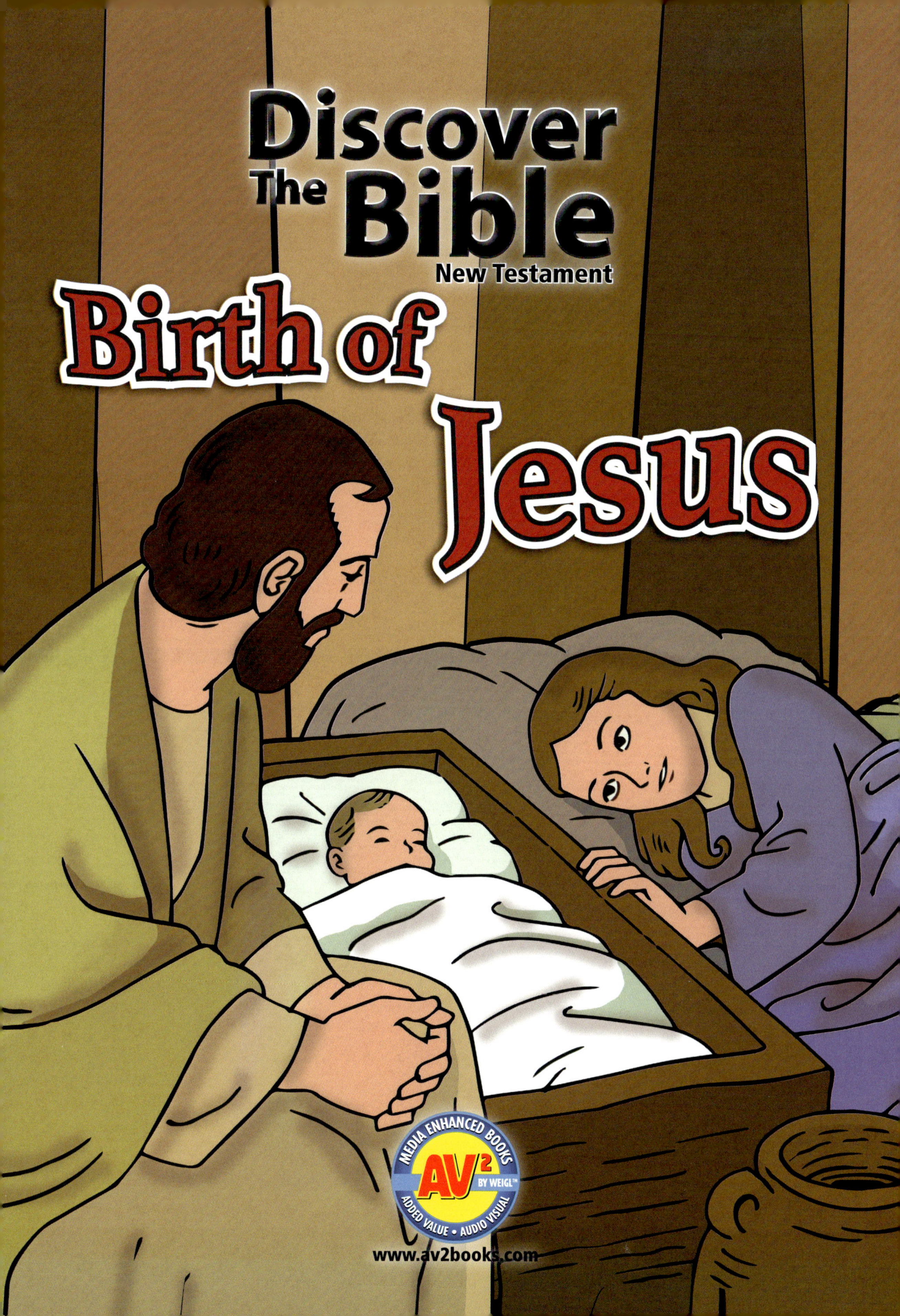
Discover
The Bible
New Testament
Birth of
Jesus
MEDIA ENHANCED BOOKS
AV2
BY WEIGL
ADDED VALUE • AUDIO VISUAL
www.av2books.com

Go to www.av2books.com, and enter this book's unique code.

BOOK CODE

AVR56278

AV² by Weigl brings you media enhanced books that support active learning.

AV² provides enriched content that supplements and complements this book. Weigl's AV² books strive to create inspired learning and engage young minds in a total learning experience.

Your AV² Media Enhanced books come alive with...

Audio
Listen to sections of the book read aloud.

Video
Watch informative video clips.

Embedded Weblinks
Gain additional information for research.

Try This!
Complete activities and hands-on experiments.

Key Words
Study vocabulary, and complete a matching word activity.

Quizzes
Test your knowledge.

Slide Show
View images and captions, and prepare a presentation.

... and much, much more!

Published by AV² by Weigl
350 5th Avenue, 59th Floor
New York, NY 10118

Website: www.av2books.com

Library of Congress Control Number: 2018941649

ISBN 978-1-4896-7283-4 (Hardcover)
ISBN 978-1-4896-7759-4 (Softcover)
ISBN 978-1-4896-7284-1 (Multi-user eBook)

Printed in the United States of America in Brainerd, Minnesota
1 2 3 4 5 6 7 8 9 0 22 21 20 19 18

072018
120817

Project Coordinator: Sara Cucini
Layout: Sushant Deshpande

Contents

Annunciation of the Birth 4

Birth of Jesus 6

Visit of the Wise Men of the East 8

Childhood of Jesus 10

Baptism of Jesus 12

Temptations of Jesus 14

Call of the Disciples 16

Wedding at Cana 20

Sermon on the Mount: The Beatitudes 22

Sermon on the Mount: Love Your Enemies 24

Sermon on the Mount: The Prayer 26

Activities 28

Annunciation of the Birth

MARY GOT READY AND HURRIED OFF TO A TOWN IN THE HILL COUNTRY OF JUDAEA.
MY COUSIN ELIZABETH WILL NEED MY HELP.

YOU ARE THE MOST BLESSED OF ALL WOMEN, AND BLESSED IS THE CHILD YOU BEAR! WHY SHOULD THIS GREAT THING HAPPEN TO ME, THAT MY LORD'S MOTHER COMES TO VISIT ME?

FOR AS SOON AS I HEARD YOUR GREETING, THE BABY WITHIN ME JUMPED WITH GLADNESS. HOW HAPPY YOU ARE TO BELIEVE THAT THE LORD'S MESSAGE TO YOU WILL COME TRUE!

MY HEART PRAISES THE LORD; MY SOUL IS GLAD BECAUSE OF GOD MY SAVIOR, FOR HE HAS REMEMBERED ME, HIS LOWLY SERVANT!

FROM NOW ON ALL PEOPLE WILL CALL ME HAPPY, BECAUSE OF THE GREAT THINGS THE MIGHTY GOD HAS DONE FOR ME. HIS NAME IS HOLY; FROM ONE GENERATION TO ANOTHER HE SHOWS MERCY TO THOSE WHO HONOR HIM.

Birth of Jesus

AH!
OH!
OH!

DON'T BE AFRAID! I AM HERE WITH GOOD NEWS FOR YOU, WHICH WILL BRING GREAT JOY TO ALL THE PEOPLE. THIS VERY DAY IN DAVID'S TOWN, YOUR SAVIOR WAS BORN— CHRIST THE LORD! AND THIS IS WHAT WILL PROVE IT TO YOU: YOU WILL FIND A BABY WRAPPED IN CLOTHS AND LYING IN A MANGER.

LET'S GO TO BETHLEHEM AND SEE THIS THING THAT HAS HAPPENED, WHICH THE LORD HAS TOLD US.

THEY FOUND THE COUPLE AND TOLD MARY WHAT THE ANGEL HAD SAID ABOUT HER NEWBORN CHILD.

MARY HEARD THEIR WORDS AND THOUGHT DEEPLY ABOUT THEM.

Visit of the Wise Men of the East

HEROD WILL BE LOOKING FOR THE CHILD IN ORDER TO KILL HIM. SO GET UP, TAKE THE CHILD AND HIS MOTHER, AND ESCAPE TO EGYPT. AND STAY THERE TILL I TELL YOU TO LEAVE.

THE WISE MEN DISAPPEARED? THIS ISN'T OVER! GO TO BETHLEHEM AND TO ALL THE SURROUNDING COUNTRYSIDE, AND KILL ALL THE MALE CHILDREN FROM TWO YEARS AND UNDER!

AFTER HEROD DIED, AN ANGEL OF THE LORD APPEARED IN A DREAM TO JOSEPH.

TAKE THE CHILD AND HIS MOTHER, AND GO BACK TO THE LAND OF ISRAEL, BECAUSE THOSE WHO TRIED TO KILL THE CHILD ARE DEAD.

IT IS SAID THAT NOW HEROD'S SON REIGNS IN JUDAEA. WE HAD BETTER MOVE TO GALILEE, FAR FROM HIS INFLUENCE.

Childhood of Jesus

OH!

JESUS WAS SITTING WITH THE JEWISH TEACHERS, LISTENING TO THEM AND ASKING QUESTIONS. ALL WHO HEARD HIM WERE AMAZED AT HIS INTELLIGENT ANSWERS.

SON, WHY HAVE YOU DONE THIS TO US? YOUR FATHER AND I HAVE BEEN WORRIED TRYING TO FIND YOU.

WHY DID YOU HAVE TO LOOK FOR ME? DIDN'T YOU KNOW THAT I HAD TO BE IN MY FATHER'S HOUSE?

SO JESUS WENT BACK WITH THEM TO NAZARETH, WHERE HE WAS OBEDIENT TO THEM. HIS MOTHER TREASURED ALL THESE THINGS IN HER HEART. JESUS GREW BOTH IN BODY AND IN WISDOM, GAINING FAVOR WITH GOD AND PEOPLE.

Baptism of Jesus

I OUGHT TO BE BAPTIZED BY YOU, AND YET YOU HAVE COME TO ME!

LET IT BE SO FOR NOW, FOR IN THIS WAY WE SHALL DO ALL THAT GOD REQUIRES.

YOU ARE MY OWN DEAR SON. I AM PLEASED WITH YOU.

I SAW THE SPIRIT COME DOWN LIKE A DOVE FROM HEAVEN AND STAY ON HIM. I HAVE SEEN IT, AND I TELL YOU THAT HE IS THE SON OF GOD.

Temptations of Jesus

THE SCRIPTURE SAYS, "GOD WILL GIVE ORDERS TO HIS ANGELS ABOUT YOU; THEY WILL HOLD YOU UP WITH THEIR HANDS, SO THAT NOT EVEN YOUR FEET WILL BE HURT ON THE STONES."

THE SCRIPTURE ALSO SAYS, "DO NOT PUT THE LORD YOUR GOD TO THE TEST."

THEN THE DEVIL TOOK JESUS TO A VERY HIGH MOUNTAIN.
I WILL GIVE YOU ALL THIS POWER AND ALL THIS WEALTH. ALL THIS WILL BE YOURS IF YOU WORSHIP ME.

GO AWAY, SATAN! THE SCRIPTURE SAYS, "WORSHIP THE LORD YOUR GOD AND SERVE ONLY HIM!"

Call of the Disciples

JAMES! JOHN! COME ON OVER AND HELP US!

GO AWAY FROM ME, LORD! I AM A SINFUL MAN!

DON'T BE AFRAID; FROM NOW ON YOU WILL BE CATCHING PEOPLE.

JESUS SAW A TAX COLLECTOR NAMED MATTHEW SITTING IN HIS OFFICE.

FOLLOW ME.

WHY DOES YOUR TEACHER EAT WITH SUCH PEOPLE?

PEOPLE WHO ARE WELL DO NOT NEED A DOCTOR, BUT ONLY THOSE WHO ARE SICK. I HAVE NOT COME TO CALL RESPECTABLE PEOPLE, BUT OUTCASTS.

PETER AND ANDREW,

JAMES AND JOHN,

PHILIP AND BARTHOLOMEW,

THOMAS AND MATTHEW,

JAMES OF ALPHAEUS, SIMON THE PATRIOT,

THADDAEUS, AND JUDAS ISCARIOT.

THE TWELVE OF YOU WILL BE NAMED APOSTLES. FROM NOW ON, YOU WILL BE WITH ME. I WILL SEND YOU OUT TO PREACH AND I WILL GIVE YOU AUTHORITY TO HEAL EVERY DISEASE AND EVERY SICKNESS.

Wedding at Cana

DO WHATEVER HE TELLS YOU.

FILL THESE JARS WITH WATER.

DRAW SOME WATER OUT AND TAKE IT TO THE MAN IN CHARGE OF THE FEAST.

MMMMM!

EVERYONE ELSE SERVES THE BEST WINE FIRST, AND AFTER THE GUESTS HAVE DRUNK A LOT, HE SERVES THE ORDINARY WINE. BUT YOU HAVE KEPT THE BEST WINE UNTIL NOW!

Sermon on the Mount: The Beatitudes

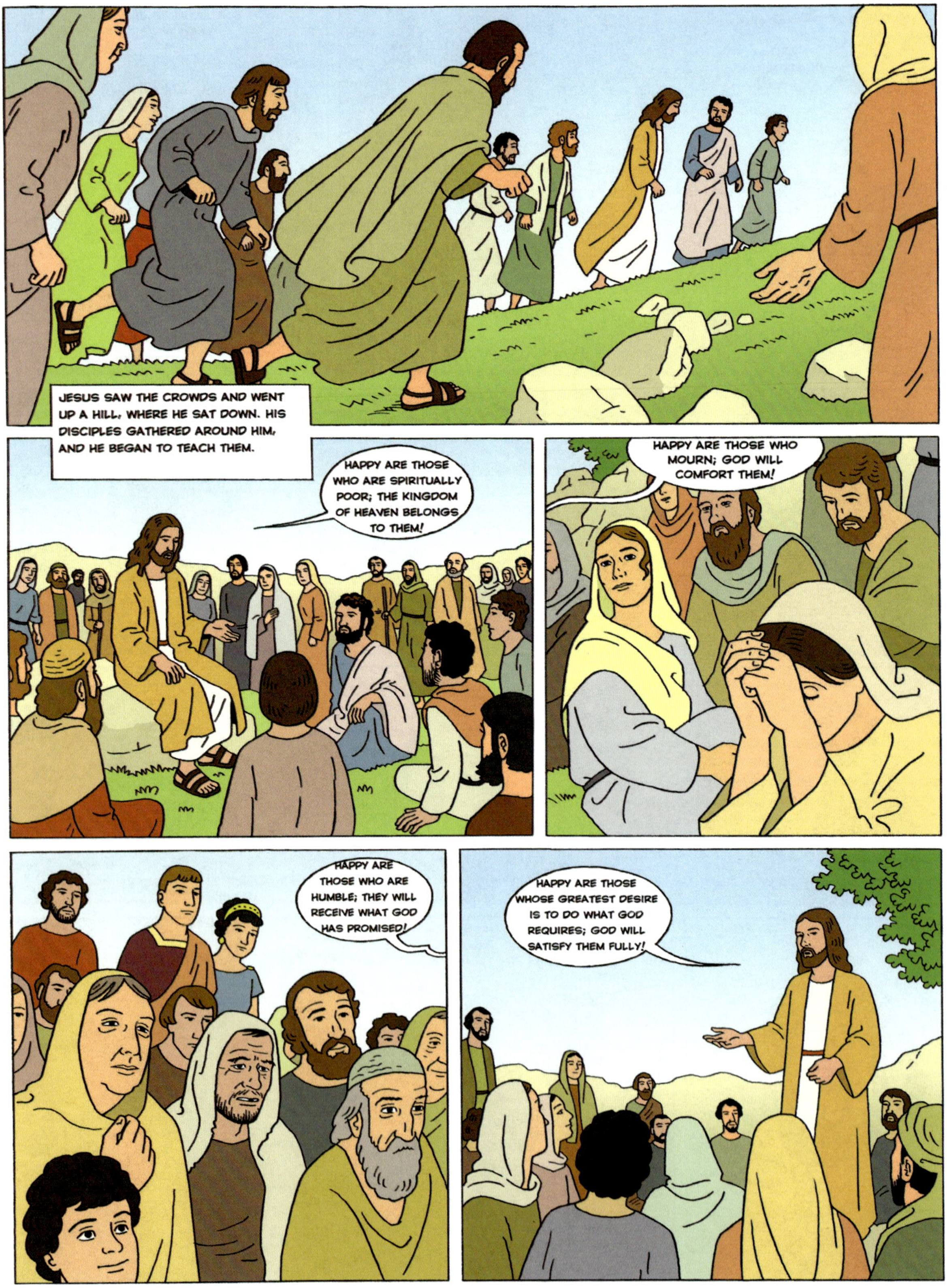

JESUS SAW THE CROWDS AND WENT UP A HILL, WHERE HE SAT DOWN. HIS DISCIPLES GATHERED AROUND HIM, AND HE BEGAN TO TEACH THEM.

HAPPY ARE THOSE WHO ARE SPIRITUALLY POOR; THE KINGDOM OF HEAVEN BELONGS TO THEM!

HAPPY ARE THOSE WHO MOURN; GOD WILL COMFORT THEM!

HAPPY ARE THOSE WHO ARE MERCIFUL TO OTHERS; GOD WILL BE MERCIFUL TO THEM!

HAPPY ARE THE PURE IN HEART; THEY WILL SEE GOD!

HAPPY ARE THOSE WHO WORK FOR PEACE; GOD WILL CALL THEM HIS CHILDREN!

HAPPY ARE THOSE WHO ARE PERSECUTED FOR DOING WHAT GOD REQUIRES; THE KINGDOM OF HEAVEN BELONGS TO THEM!

HAPPY ARE YOU WHEN PEOPLE INSULT YOU AND PERSECUTE YOU AND TELL ALL KINDS OF EVIL LIES AGAINST YOU BECAUSE YOU ARE MY FOLLOWERS. BE HAPPY AND GLAD, FOR A GREAT REWARD IS KEPT FOR YOU IN HEAVEN!

Sermon on the Mount: Love Your Enemies

YOU HAVE HEARD IT SAID, "LOVE YOUR FRIENDS, HATE YOUR ENEMIES."

BUT NOW I TELL YOU: LOVE YOUR ENEMIES AND PRAY FOR THOSE WHO PERSECUTE YOU. DO FOR OTHERS JUST WHAT YOU WANT THEM TO DO FOR YOU.

IF YOU LOVE ONLY THE PEOPLE WHO LOVE YOU, WHY SHOULD YOU RECEIVE A BLESSING? EVEN SINNERS LOVE THOSE WHO LOVE THEM!

NO! LOVE YOUR ENEMIES AND DO GOOD TO THEM. YOU WILL THEN HAVE A GREAT REWARD, AND YOU WILL BE CHILDREN OF THE MOST HIGH GOD. FOR HE IS GOOD TO THE UNGRATEFUL AND THE WICKED.

BE MERCIFUL JUST AS YOUR FATHER IS MERCIFUL.

Sermon on the Mount: The Prayer

DO NOT BE WORRIED ABOUT FOOD AND DRINK, OR ABOUT CLOTHES. YOUR FATHER IN HEAVEN KNOWS THAT YOU NEED ALL THESE THINGS. SEEK THE KINGDOM OF GOD AND DO WHAT HE REQUIRES OF YOU, AND HE WILL PROVIDE YOU WITH ALL THESE OTHER THINGS.
DO NOT WORRY ABOUT TOMORROW; IT WILL HAVE ENOUGH WORRIES OF ITS OWN. THERE IS NO NEED TO ADD TO THE TROUBLES EACH DAY BRINGS.
ASK, AND YOU WILL RECEIVE; SEEK, AND YOU WILL FIND; KNOCK, AND THE DOOR WILL BE OPENED TO YOU. FOR EVERYONE WHO ASKS WILL RECEIVE, AND ANYONE WHO SEEKS WILL FIND.
WOULD ANY OF YOU WHO ARE FATHERS GIVE YOUR SON A STONE WHEN HE ASKS FOR BREAD? AS BAD AS YOU ARE, YOU KNOW HOW TO GIVE GOOD THINGS TO YOUR CHILDREN. HOW MUCH MORE, THEN, WILL YOUR FATHER IN HEAVEN GIVE GOOD THINGS TO THOSE WHO ASK HIM!
WHEN JESUS FINISHED SAYING THESE THINGS, THE CROWDS WERE AMAZED AT THE WAY HE TAUGHT. HE WASN'T LIKE THE TEACHERS OF THE LAW; INSTEAD, HE TAUGHT WITH AUTHORITY.

Find the Differences

The crowd followed Jesus to listen to him.
The images on pages 28–30 seem identical, but there are seven differences in each pair. Can you spot them all?

Find the Differences

Activity

Find the Differences

Spot the Children

Seven children are in the crowd listening to the words of Jesus. Can you find them all?

Log on to www.av2books.com

AV² by Weigl brings you media enhanced books that support active learning. Go to www.av2books.com, and enter the special code found on page 2 of this book. You will gain access to enriched and enhanced content that supplements and complements this book. Content includes video, audio, weblinks, quizzes, a slide show, and activities.

AV² Online Navigation

Audio
Listen to sections of the book read aloud.

Book Pages
AV² pages directly correspond to pages in the book.

Video
Watch informative video clips.

Embedded Weblinks
Gain additional information for research.

Key Words
Study vocabulary, and complete a matching word activity.

Try This!
Complete activities and hands-on experiments.

Quizzes
Test your knowledge.

Slide Show
View images and captions, and prepare a presentation.

AV² was built to bridge the gap between print and digital. We encourage you to tell us what you like and what you want to see in the future.

Sign up to be an AV² Ambassador at www.av2books.com/ambassador.

Due to the dynamic nature of the Internet, some of the URLs and activities provided as part of AV² by Weigl may have changed or ceased to exist. AV² by Weigl accepts no responsibility for any such changes. All media enhanced books are regularly monitored to update addresses and sites in a timely manner. Contact AV² by Weigl at 1-866-649-3445 or av2books@weigl.com with any questions, comments, or feedback.